FRENCH CANAJAN, HÉ?

MARK M. ORKIN

Illustrations by Isaac Bickerstaff

*To Mom +
Dad
From Heather
Christmas 1976*

Lester and Orpen Limited

Also by Mark M. Orkin

Canajan, Eh?
Speaking Canadian English
Speaking Canadian French
Legal Ethics
The Law of Costs

ISBN 0-919630-01-4
Printed in Canada.

Remémoration d'amis québecois.

Je vis de bonne soupe et non de beau langage.
Molière

INTRODUCTION

For a long time now it has been common practice to divide the population of Canada into two groups: the Anglophones and the Francophones.[1] In recent years these expressions have become so familiar that one might be forgiven for assuming that the majority of the population — the Anglophones — speak English, while the remainder — the Francophones — speak French. In fact, as we shall see, nothing could be further from the truth.

It is not even clear how these two expressions originated. According to one theory they are modifications of two earlier terms which go back to a remote era when Canada was divided into two groups, the Anglophobes or English haters, and the Francophobes or French haters. These relate to a time, fortunately long past, when differences of opinion were commonly settled on the battlefield. The fact that we live in more enlightened times should not blind us to the strong feelings of our ancestors.

What historical forces brought about the transformation of these primitive terms of social conflict into the more manageable

---

[1]It may be here noted that division is one of the chief characteristics of the Canajan ethos. Thus we often hear it said that Great Britain consists of England, Scotland and Wales; the U.S.A. is made up of 50 states; the U.S.S.R. is composed of 15 constituent republics, and so on. By contrast, Canada is divided into 10 provinces.

expressions Anglophone and Francophone? No one is certain. And may we expect that some day the process of social evolution will refine the present terms into Anglophil and Francophil? Only time will tell.[1]

For our purposes, however, we shall concentrate on Phase Two of this cultural progression. And our thesis may be simply stated. It is that for Canada the expressions Anglophone and Francophone no longer have any meaning.

While this may appear paradoxical at first, a moment's reflection will demonstrate its truth. Some years ago the federal government passed a law making English and French the official languages of Canada. Did this legislative enactment make all Canadians speak either English or French? Quite the contrary. Fewer people speak these languages today than before the law was passed. Indeed, both official languages have been declining for years and we may confidently expect that, as they become optional subjects in our schools, they will die out completely. Parents can verify this by listening to their children for a change.

The fallacy of trying to legislate human conduct is, of course, familiar to students of social history. The 18th Amendment to the

[1]At this point students of Claude Lévi-Strauss will recognize echoes of his binary approach to cultural anthropology. Clearly what is good enough for the jungles of Brazil will also do for the shores of the St. Lawrence.

U.S. constitution was enacted to make people stop drinking liquor. As is well known, the experiment failed. Indeed, just the opposite result was achieved. In the same way, any attempt to make Canadians speak either English or French is also foredoomed to failure. To make them speak both would, of course, be beyond the competence of any terrestrial authority.

This does not mean, however, that Canadians will be reduced to using sign language. Rather, with the inevitable decline of English and French, the two folk languages — Canajan for Anglos and joual for Kay Beckers — will at last come into their own.

That day may not be far distant. For generations our schools have tried to teach English and French, but each year, as any teacher can testify, fewer and fewer children speak or write these dying languages. On the other hand our schools have either ignored or tried to stamp out Canajan and joual for generations, and yet today they are flourishing as never before.

Elsewhere we have examined some of the ramifications of Canajan. Our purpose here is to consider the spread and scope of joual, whose importance has been consistently underrated at every level of government and throughout the educational system.

One example will suffice. Not long ago the ruling political party in Kay Beck embarked on a well-publicized campaign to make French *la langue de travail*, the language of work. An election was even won on the issue. But later the campaign was quietly dropped when it was discovered that practically nobody in the province spoke French any more. After long study a Language Commission reported that the workers spoke Canajan to the boss and joual among themselves. As for French, as one respondent observed: *'Perle-moé s'en pâ!'* and another: *'Toute la gang est comme çâ icitte. On s'comprind.'* And a third: *'Ta yeule! Moé non pus.'*[1]

It is in ignorance of these basic facts of linguistic life that politicians of every shade are blindly going about the business of promoting (or opposing) bilingualism when in fact the issue (along with bilingualism) died some time ago. If, as independent scientific tests have shown, some 9 out of 10 Canadians no longer speak either English or French, then any campaign to expand (or restrict) the use of these languages is more than futile.[2] For the time is fast approaching in Canada when English and French

[1] For the meaning of these and other terms the reader is invited to consult the glossary which follows.

[2] The true state of affairs was inadvertently revealed by the census of 1971. In answer to the question 'What language do you most often speak at home?' 5,546,025 respondents said that it wasn't English, while 14,446,235 respondents said it wasn't French. In other words, if one adds these figures one perceives the astounding fact that 19,992,260 out of 21,568,310 Canajans —

words will have to be marked with the lexicographer's asterisk in front of them, to indicate a hypothetical or presumed word. So the next generation of dictionaries may well show *Lake Huron followed by the Canajan term 'Lake Urine '[1] or *maudit where the correct or joual expression is *moe dzee*.[2]

The brief survey of joual which follows has been prepared to help clarify some of these matters. And since no language can properly be viewed in the abstract, an attempt will be made to show joual in its social and historical contexts. It cannot be emphasized too strongly, however, that the present work is not intended as a teaching aid. Otherwise its title would be something like *Joual Self-Taught*, which is a contradiction in terms since no evidence whatever exists that joual can be the subject of any

more than 92.6 per cent of the total population — didn't speak either English or French at home! The census takers were careful not to ask the most important question of all, but the answer is self-evident: the language that all those people did speak at home was either joual or Canajan. By not asking one question the census takers effectively suppressed this vital information which appears here for the first time.

[1]According to environmentalists this Canajan expression is thought to have reference to ecological damage caused to the Grade Lakes system by the Mare Cans, but the exact linkage has yet to be shown etymologically.

[2]For a discussion of *moe dzee* in its eponymous sense, *vide infra*.

known method of language instruction. In fact, as noted above, educators in Kay Beck have spent most of their time trying to get people to unlearn joual. In vain, for it appears that joual can be neither taught nor untaught. Like its sister language, Canajan, it simply is.

And like Canajan its dominant qualities include a plethora of pleonasms and a fatality of accidence. As will appear, joual is prone to catechresis and prodelision, while xenogamy is pandemic. Tmesis, however, rarely occurs. As we have seen in an earlier study, these are precisely the characteristics of Canajan.

A closer analysis than time and space permit would reveal the existence of isobars which dichotomize both folk languages. Thus joual may initially be divided into *haut joual* and *bas joual*, just as Canajan falls into the two broad divisions of upper Canajan and lower Canajan. It should be stressed, however, that we are speaking here in socio-linguistic terms, so that this taxonomy owes nothing to the traditional political divisions of Upper Canada and Lower Canada which, in any case, have to do with the way the land slopes. Clearly much work remains to be done in this unploughed field, some of which will emerge in the pages that follow.

A final word should be said about grammar. French without tears? — barely possible. French without rules? — unthinkable.

Indeed, it may not be too much to assert that French *is* rules, and nothing more. Remove the rules and the once proud French language would dissolve in a puff of diacritic signs. Hence the dictum attributed to Vaugelas in his *Remarques* (1647): 'No rules, no French.'

From this follows the charge so often brought against joual that it is without rules; that its parents, being reputedly unmarried, could confer no legal status on their offspring; that it has no visible means of support. This type of *a priori* reasoning has long marked the official attitude toward the people's language: since it has no rules it does not exist.

But with the growth of joual studies at some of our institutions of lower learning, it is becoming apparent that joual has indeed rules; that they are as rigorous as those of Standard French; and that they endow the people's language with all the legitimation that the purest purist could demand. Some of these rules will be enunciated in the text, and others left to the reader's imagination.

A PERSONAL NOTE

The Canada Council having let me down a second time, I am once more obliged to revert to the days of my extreme youth in order to ascribe responsibility for this salutary work.

My first encounter with joual goes back to a time many years ago when, as a boy in Ottawa, I used to clerk after school in my father's bakeshop. One day a boy even smaller than I came into the shop and, upon being asked what he wanted, demanded to have something that sounded like *'san sett de galette.'* His request seemed incomprehensible to me and we looked at each other for a long moment, unable to communicate further.

Fortunately my mother, who was standing near by, had learned her good provincial French in Belgium, so that her ear had not been perverted by the rigours of the standard language. Without a moment's hesitation she grasped that what the boy wanted was a nickel's worth of yesterday's cookies. These were soon forthcoming and a sale was concluded to the satisfaction of both parties.

It was on subsequent occasions and in other circumstances that I first made the acquaintance of *moe dzee* and many other terms not to be found in any standard dictionary.

Typically, our first response to such words was puzzlement.

Long afterwards, when we discovered that they were looked down on by the teaching establishment, we copied the same attitude — we who, after four years of high-school French, were incapable of carrying on the simplest conversation in anything approaching the international or, for that matter, any standard.

Far too much time has been spent by too many people trying to show where the French language went wrong in Canada. Indeed, the favourite descriptive words invoked by the Linguistic Purity League have traditionally been *déformations, impropriétés* and *barbarismes*. So in the sentence quoted above one might begin by demonstrating that International French *cinq* [sɛ̃ːk] has in Canada come to be pronounced without the final /k/ as [sɛ̃] and so on, but what would be the point of the exercise? We should have found the trees, but lost the forest.

We at least had youth to justify our error. Responding from ignorance rather than linguistic perception, we failed to realize that we were listening to a different language. We laughed and thought it bad French. We were wrong: in fact, it was good joual.

A

A

She. Pronounce to rhyme with 'blah.' In joual the personal pronouns are much syncopated. She and he are *a* and *y* respectively. As in: *a m'dzit* (in Canajan: 'sh'tole me'); *y est* (in Canajan: 'heeze'). When *a* occurs before a word beginning with a vowel, the form *alle* is preferred. Thus: *alle est* (in Canajan: 'sheeze'). For a fuller discussion of personal pronouns see *Moé*. Cf. French **elle*.[1]

ADIDOU!

There is no exact joual equivalent for the Canajan salutational greeting 'Harya!', usage being divided between *Adidou!* and *Allô!* Like 'Harya!' both terms are free from the excessive formalism of the standard language which requires a high degree of punctillio in these matters (*Enchanté de faire votre connaissance*, etc.). Indeed, *Allô!* verges on *bas joual*, roughly approximating lower Canajan 'Hi!'

---

[1]As noted (see *Introduction*) lexicographers use the sign * to indicate a presumed or hypothetical etymological form. Here it is used to signal the Standard French form of a joual word or phrase, which is usually a presumed or hypothetical form so far as joual speakers are concerned.

17

Some linguists have purported to uncover in both *Adidou!* and 'Harya!' a buried enquiry about the state of health or well-being of the addressee, even going so far as to propound the *ur*-forms **how-do-you-do* and **how-are-you*. But this is pure speculation and, even if it were true, long and hard use has worn both expressions smooth of such connotations. Thus, the most commonly accepted response to each is simply a repetition of the initial greeting. The idiomatic answer to *Adidou!* is *Adidou!*, just as one normally responds to 'Harya!' with 'Harya!'

Usage is, however, roomy enough to accommodate even those purists who insist upon replying to an unasked question. So it is not unidiomatic to answer *Adidou!* with *pâ si pire*, just as one may reply to 'Harya!' with 'priddy good.'

A third opening gambit may be offered with the expression *çâ vâ?* (pronounced something like 'saw vaw'). Here again usage customarily requires an echoic response. Accordingly, the ideal encounter should run somewhat as follows. First speaker: *'çâ vâ?'* Second speaker: *'çâ vâ.'* The tone of the response will serve to convey the second speaker's meaning. This may range all the way from *'çâ vâ'* (up beat) through *'çâ vâ'* (resigned) to *'çâ vâ'* (despondent).

As with *Adidou!* pedants have sought to read into *çâ vâ?* an inquiry as to the addressee's state of health, etc., but this theory is almost certainly negated by the omission of the prefatory word *comment*. However, even here usage permits as a reply to *'çâ vâ?'* the mildly informative *'çâ vâ ben, pis vous?'*

The parting salutations in joual are likewise less rigid than those available in the standard language which are renowned both for periphrasis and insincerity. Even the least formal of the French terms, *au revoir*, obliges the speaker, regardless of his true feelings, to look forward with implied pleasure to the next encounter with his opposite number. By contrast a joual speaker avoids both prolixity and hypocrisy through use of the brief and neutral *Bébail* (pronounced 'bay-bye'). As with *çâ vâ*, any desired emotional component can be supplied by tonal variations.

ALLÔ!

Hi! See *Adidou!* Cf. French *bonjour*.

AMIE DE FILLE

Girlfriend. See *Tchomme*. Cf. French *amie*.

ANÉOUÉ

In any case; at any rate. Pronounce something like 'annie whey.'
As in: *Anéoué y est pâ v'nu* (in Canajan: 'Anyways he dint
come'). Cf. French *de toute façon*.

ANGLO

Anglos are one of the two found-in races, according to the Bye
and Bye Commission. The word may be defined in various ways
according to the angle of observation. Thus, ethnically, an Anglo
is simply a non-French Canajan Canajan. Linguistically he is a
non-joual speaker. Politically, at least in popular belief, an Anglo
is a member of the former ruling minority in Kay Beck.
Ornithologically an Anglo is an easily-recognized bird —
colouring red, white and blue; habitat Westmount; mates on
Dominion Day.

 Despite the look of the word, an Anglo is neither an
Englishman nor a person of English extraction,[1] although both are
comprised in the term, nor even (but we are getting warmer) an
Anglophone.

 Anglo is not to be confused with Anglo-Saxon. A recent

---

[1] In keeping with a country largely devoted to extractive industries, Canajans are
themselves extracted from many other lands.

immgrunt from Iddly who doesn't want to send his children to a French language school is an Anglo.

In Kay Beck the term Anglo is one of those key words which fix, at one and the same time, the definer and the defined, as well as the society in which they co-exist. Like most joual (and, indeed, Canajan) words of this category, Anglo conveys what is essentially a negative concept. No exact translation exists, but a fairly accurate version might be 'not canadzien' or, more freely, 'not one of us.' In its only affirmative sense *les Anglos* means simply 'Them.'

Elsewhere we have seen that the least praiseworthy expression in the Canajan lexicon is Mare Can, signifying pollution, corruption, oppression, economic and political take-over, and so on. As such it has long been the favourite rallying-cry of all right-thinking Canajans.

Among French Canajans, however, the cognate term is Anglo to denote pollution, corruption, oppression, economic and political take-over, and so on. According to joual folklore, the Anglos are responsible for every social ill which afflicts Kay Beck from bad breath to pot-holes in the roads. So firmly is this notion entrenched that the Mare Cans are actually blamed for very little in Kay Beck, thus permitting them to pollute, corrupt, oppress, and take over economically and politically almost without hindrance.

ANGLOTERRE

See *Deux Nations*.

ASSISEZ-VOUS

Rule 9, *q.v.*, which requires that all joual verbs be irregular, applies not only to verbs which are regular in Standard French but also to verbs which are already irregular in the standard language. However, joual verbs are irregular in their own way.

A good example is provided by *asseoir*, a verb which traditionally has lived a most irregular life in France. As is well-known, the second person plural imperative is *asseyez-vous*. One would think this form irregular enough for most tastes, but not for joual which instead requires the form *assisez-vous* (in Canajan: 'siddown!').

A small point, perhaps, but those who think that joual has no rules would do well to remember it.

ASTEUR

At the present time, now, nowadays. As in: *les gens d'asteur* (in Canajan: 'peepla t'day'). Cf. French *à cette heure*, *maintenant*.

ATCHOUMER

To sneeze. Cf. French *éternuer*.
The substantive is *atchoum!*

A - *TCHOUM!*

SIR WILFRID LAURIER

AUSSI

Either. As in: *'Tsu va pâ? Moé aussi'* (in Canajan: 'Yer not goin? Me either'). Cf. French *non plus*. See also *itou*.

AUTE

Other, another. Pronounce to rhyme with 'goat.' As in: *les aute deux* (in Canajan: 'the both of them'). Cf. French *les deux autres*.

AVÉ

With, by means of. As in: *frappe-lé avé l'bâton!* (in Canajan: 'Hiddim with tha [hockey] stick!'). Cf. French *avec*.

AVOUÉRE

Joual auxiliary verb 'to have.' Pronounce to rhyme more or less with 'have wire.' Although *avouére* is generally conjugated like French *avoir*, some distinctive forms may be noted, among them: *j'avons ben gros d'travail* (in Canajan: 'I godda lodda work'). Cf. French *J'ai beaucoup de travail*. Also: *a'vous vu mon crayon?* (in Canajan: 'Didja see my pentzel?') Cf. French *avez-vous vu*, etc.

RULE 1. When In Doubt, Leave It Out.

Joual avoids the flourishes, furbelows and curlicues which make up the glory of Standard French. Therein lies its unique merit. Not for joual the pluperfect subjunctive and past periphrastic tenses, the partitive rules or the pleonastic *ne*. The reason is simple. During the period when joual first began to develop, the people of Kay Beck were too poor to afford such extravagances. Life was hard and there was no room for luxury in Nooph Rance. Consequently the folk language grew up stunted and half-starved, with all its bones showing.

Dire necessity decreed that everything which was not absolutely essential had to go. This was the first rule. What remained became joual.

Once we understand that joual was built by leaving things out, we are well on the way to getting the hang of it. We also realize why members of the teaching establishment have always set their faces sternly against the people's language. It is so basic, who needs teachers?

Thus reduction forms the essence of joual. Consider by way of example the first person pronoun. Everyone is familiar with the difference between the noisy, bragging English 'I' and the quiet French '*je*' whose lower-case initial letter offers a glimpse into a whole world of self-assurance. Joual, on the other hand, subjugates the ego by reducing it to a whispered '*j*' as in *j's'rai* (in Canajan: 'Allbee'); *J'vas aller chercher* (in Canajan: 'Allgo C').

Indeed, the French Canajan 'I' may disappear from sight altogether in a mixture of mashed potatoes (*pétaques machées*) and self-abnegation: thus, the form *chus* equals *je suis*.

This process of lopping and chopping which is going on all the time in joual proceeds through the other personal pronouns and, as we shall have the occasion to see, out into the vocabulary of daily life. It thus corresponds precisely to the unbridled apheresis, syncope and apocope of Canajan which we have examined in a previous study.

B

BADLOQUE

Term signifying adversity or misfortune. Pronounce 'bad lock.' As in: *Y a d'la badloque* (in Canajan: 'Heeze owda luck'). The adjectival form is *badloqué*. Cf. French **malchance*, **malchanceux*.

BÂDRER

One of the all-time joual greats, *bâdrer* has a long and
distinguished history stretching back into the dim past of
ur-joual. Pronounce 'boh dray' where the first syllable lies
somewhere between 'bow' and 'baw.'

    It would be oversimplifying things to say that *bâdrer* means
merely 'to bother' although this is its primary signification, as in:
bâdrez-moé pâ (in Canajan: 'Doan bother me'). For at least a
dozen French verbs are required to convey its range of meaning:
*gêner, *ennuyer, *fatiguer, *déranger, *tracasser, etc. *Bâdrer*
thus affords a good example of the economy of joual, the art of
making one word do for many, the plain for the high-sounding,
the simple for the recondite. See Rule 1.

    Yet despite its simplicity, *bâdrer* has spawned a multiplicity
of forms, of which it is sufficient to mention in passing the
adjective *bâdrant*, as in: *C'est une parsonne bâdrante* (in
Canajan: 'Sheeza bothersome indivijul'), and the noun *bâdreux*,
as in: *C'est un bâdreux* (in Canajan: 'Heeza pest').

BEN

A mild intensive. Pronounce with the nasalized sound of *vingt*.
As in: *C'est ben simple* (in Canajan: 'Seezy'); *'coute ben* (in
Canajan: 'Lisseneer'); *A l'aime ben çâ* (in Canajan: 'Shlikes it

lots'). Cf. French *bien.

BEN BEN

Stronger than *ben*. *Ben* squared. As in: *C'est pâ ben ben bon* (in Canajan: 'Snotso good').

BEN OUAI

Affirmative response to a question. The Canajan equivalent is 'shir.' Thus: *'Tsu veux m'accompagner?' 'Ben ouai'* (in Canajan: 'Yawanna come?' 'Shir').

BEN'VNUE

The customary response to an expression of thanks. First speaker: *'Marci beaucoup.'* Second speaker: *'Ben'vnue'* (in Canajan: First speaker: 'Thang slot.' Second speaker: 'Dough men schnitt'). Cf. French *il n'y a pas de quoi.

BITTER

To beat, to get the better of. Pronounce 'bit eh.' As in: *çâ m'bitte* (in Canajan: 'Beet smee'). From this comes the adjective *bittable* or, more properly, *bittab'*, as in: *Y est pâ bittab'* (in Canajan: 'Ya canned beadim'). Cf. French *dépasser.

B'LINGUE

Gay. Pronounce the second syllable with the nasal sound of *vingt*.
As in: *Y est b'lingue* (in Canajan: 'Heeze wunna tha boys').

In Kay Beck *b'lingue* is one of those words which genteel
lexicographers sometimes mark with a warning sign like ⚓
meaning 'watch out!' or 'handle with care!' It is not to be
confused with *bilingue* (in Canajan: 'bling yule'), although the
latter is a word many Kay Beckers prefer to stay away from these
days, and which should perhaps also be marked with its own ⚓.

BLOC

Block or street. As in: *Y est à deux blocs d'icitte* (in Canajan: 'Stoo blocks fra mere'). Cf. French **Il est à deux rues* (or *coins de rue*) *d'ici*.

BÓFFLÒ

City in Les États, *q.v.*, noted for its Canajan hockey team.

BOMMER

To loaf, to bum around. Pronounce rather like 'bow may.' In spite of its indolence, *bommer* has managed to spawn quite a verbal progeny, including the noun *bommeur*, the adjective *bommeux*, and the verbal phrase *ét' sur la bomme*, to be on the bum. Cf. French **flâner* which is, however, a pallid substitute.

BON YEU

A mild joual expletive, of slightly less intensity than *Mon Dou!* About the wattage of Heavens to Betsy!

BOSTER

To break or burst. As in: *La pipe est bostée* (in Canajan: 'The pipe busted'). Cf. French **éclater*.

C

ÇÂ

A multi-purpose pronoun in joual. Pronounce rather like 'saw' but with a short rather than a drawled 'aw' sound.

Çâ has a dozen meanings of which the commonest are 'it' and 'that.' As in: *çâ nége* (in Canajan: 'It's knowing'); *J'veux pâ çâ* (in Canajan: 'Eye dough wannit').

CANADÂ

In the immediately following entry we will try to distinguish between the terms *canadzien* and Canajan, and the reader is directed there for a discussion of the etymological and semantic considerations involved.

For present purposes it is sufficient to say that the same difference exists between the substantives *Canadâ* and Canada as between the forms *canadzien* and Canajan, and for much the same reasons.

Pronounce like 'Cana-daw' but don't drawl the 'aw' sound.

CANADZIEN

A lexicographer might be tempted to define this word as: 'a. & n. (Native) of Canada,' but he would be wrong.

CANADZIEN : JACQUES GODBOUT, JACQUES FERRON, ROCH CARRIER, MARIE CLAIRE-BLAIS, ANNE HÉBERT

Nor is the joual term *canadzien* to be equated with the familiar word 'Canajan.' Some authorities believe that the two expressions have a common etymological root, but the connection is obscure and not easily demonstrated. Their meanings, in any case, are quite different, although the distinction may seem a subtle one.

When a Kay Becker uses the word *canadzien*, it is true that he means 'Canadian,' but in his mind the term refers only to himself and his friends; everyone else is an Anglo.

Similarly, when an Anglo says Canajan, he also means 'Canadian,' but the mental picture which he forms includes only himself and *his* friends; there may be other people but he finds it easy not to think about them.

It follows that the population of the country is divided without overlapping into *canadziens* and Canajans. A person may be one or the other, but not both. Anyone who doesn't fit into either of these two categories must be an ethnic.

Recently *canadzien* is being overtaken in general usage by Kay Beckwah, but that is another story.

This all too brief exegesis leaves open larger societal problems, the answers to which lie outside the scope of the present work. A few of these problems may, however, be suggested for the guidance of future researchers:

1. Where do Indians and Eskimos fit into this scheme of things? Answer: they don't, although with the extension of television to remote areas they may very well end up just like the rest of us.

2. Can a *canadzien* make himself into a Canajan, and vice versa? Answer: probably not. In any case, why would he want to?

CAR CHAY, JOCK

In order to support the claim that the French are one of the two found-in races, Jock Car Chay (a Frenchman) insisted on discovering Canada in 1534 although it had already been discovered by John Kabow (or Kabott) in 1497, thereby making the English the earlier found-in race. Not to be deterred, however, Jock steadfastly went on and discovered the Gulpha Sen Lornz, which had already been fished out by the Portuguese fleet, and also the Sen Lornz River, which had already been discovered and settled by the Indians.

Unmoved by all this action, however, Car Chay landed at Gaspy and set up a large cross to signify that he was taking possession of the land in the name of the King of France. After the Indians offered some objection to this on the ground that it infringed on their native rights, Car Chay assured them that the

thing was actually a beacon to mark the entrance to the bay. When the Indians pointed out that they already knew where the entrance to the bay was and so didn't need a beacon, Car Chay mumbled something and told his men to get back on board ship. As so often happened in the development of Nooph Rance, the cross and the double-cross went hand in hand.

Proceeding on up the river Jock's men landed at what is now Mont Ray-all and went directly to the corner of Peel and St. Catherine Streets, which was the site of the native village of Hochelaga. There Jock fell in with a local beaver-board maker named Donnacona who told him stories about fabulous mines to be found farther up the line in the Kingdom of the Saggin, eh? It may be that Donnacona made up the story just to get rid of Car Chay and his men who had been away from home for quite a long time and were starting to eye the local girls. But whatever the case, it was Canada's first mining promotion and as such the precursor of the moose-pasture syndrome which traces its wavy way down through Canajan history like the fancy engraving on a worthless stock certificate.

As with many speculators who followed in his footsteps over the centuries, Car Chay was looking for that great gold mine in the sky. Thus he was only too willing to believe a lot of loose talk about ore bodies, mineralization, geophysical surveys, etc. and, as there was no securities legislation in Nooph Rance in those days to protect unwary investors, he got taken. Donnacona reluctantly agreed to part with many barrels of gold-bearing rock which proved worthless when it was examined back in France. The King of France was very disappointed in Jock and stopped talking to him. Not so Mrs. Car Chay, however, who didn't let him forget it for a long time.

This episode illustrates one of the great themes of Canajan history: Winning the Land and Losing Your Shirt.

Car Chay and his crew were the first white men to winter in Canada, then as now a great mistake. Without central heating or a balanced diet they suffered great hardship and many perished. They also found it strange that the ignorant savages who had not enjoyed their advantages seemed not to mind it at all, but passed their time smoking, drinking and inventing folklore. In the spring Car Chay and his men, by then a scurvy lot, sailed back to France much sadder but no wiser, and certainly no richer.

After this trying experience Car Chay wanted to discover Florida and take it easy for a while. But by now the King had lost interest completely, and besides the Spaniards had already discovered Florida where they were busy introducing the European plan. So Car Chay settled down in his home town of St. Malo and grew old and forgotten. He passed his days telling stories about his incredible adventures to the small boys of the port. In time he came to believe most of them himself and died a happy man.

ÇARTAIN

Certain, sure, to be relied upon. As in: *C'est sûr et çartain* (in Canajan: 'That's fir sure'). Pronounce to rhyme with *vingt*.

CAW SHAY

To hide. As in: *A s'est caw shay derrière l'âbe* (in Canajan: 'She hid behine tha tree'). *N.B.* pronounce *derrière* to rhyme more or less with 'wire.' Cf. French **cacher*.

CHÂR

Automobile. Pronounce half-way between 'shore' and 'shower.' Cf. French **voiture*.

The story of the *bazou* or joual jalopy is soon told. It is governed almost entirely by Rule 12, *q.v.*, from the *bompeur* (cf. French **pare-chocs*) to the *brêke* (**frein*) to the *frême* (**chassis*) to the *mofleur* (**silencieux*), yes, even unto the *plogues* (**bougies*).

Almost everything which can happen to a *bazou* — even if it be *un christ de beau châr* in the eyes of its owner — must do so in accordance with the dictates of Rule 12. Thus, on the road, a joual driver may experience something relatively minor like *un flat* (cf.

French **une crevaison*) requiring no more than a brief application of *le jack* (**le cric*) to replace the errant member with *le spére* (**la roue de secours*). Something more serious like *un trouble de moteur* (**une panne de moteur*) may call for *le touage* (**le remorquage*) in order to *overâler* (**réviser*) *le moteur*.

But if the *bazou* is *en raque* (*en ruine) nothing can be done; *y faut le scraper* (**il faut l'envoyer à la ferraille*). Such is the ineluctable logic of Rule 12.

CHRÉQUIEN

Christian (in Canajan: 'Chriss chun'). Cf. French *chrétien.

CHUS

The first person singular of the joual verb *être*, to be; thus, *chus* equals I am. Pronounce rather like 'shoe' but with the distinctive (and unpronounceable) French 'u' sound, so that it comes out a cross between 'shoe' and 'she.'

    Chus is perhaps the classic example of the application of joual Rule 1, *q.v.* To arrive at *chus* one must, following the provisions of Rule 1, take the Standard French expression *je suis and then discard every superfluous phoneme, reduce the number of monemes as far as they can go and, indeed, eliminate everthing except the original significatum or meaning. One then proceeds to construct out of fresh phonemes a new moneme having approximately the same significatum as the first expression.[1]

[1]We say 'approximately' since there are clearly differences (philosophical, psychological etc.) between joual *chus* and Standard French *je suis, but this is neither the time nor place to cut a hair in four, as the French say.

The reader may well ask at this point: Why is all this necessary when we already have at hand the familiar and widely-accepted form *je suis?* The answer is simple: Rule 1 requires it.

One word of caution. For the sake of simplicity we have treated the formation of *chus* as though it were a willed act accomplished by slavishly following a fixed rule, rather like baking a cake according to a recipe in a book. In reality *chus* is the end product of a long and complicated evolutionary process that took place over untold generations during which joual slowly arose from the ruins of Standard French much as, in the days when Rome was busy declining and falling, French itself emerged from the ashes of Latin.

The conjugation of *être* is not otherwise interesting except to the specialist, but for convenience the following paradigm sets out all that one needs to know about the subject:

Present Indicative of *être, to be*

1. Affirmative	2. Negative
I yam, etc.	*I yain't, etc.*
chus	chus pâ
t'es	t'es pâ
y est	y est pâ
nous sommes	nous sommes pâ
v'z'êtes	v'z'êtes pâ
y sont	y sont pâ

When you pronounce *être*, don't forget that the first syllable is not quite 'ite' (as in 'mite') and not quite 'ate' (as in 'mate'), but something in between the two.

There have been a number of famous *chus* in history. Perhaps the most celebrated is the Cartesian formula: *J' pinse, don' chus.*

C'MINT

How, in what way. Pronounce to rhyme with *vingt*. As in: *C'mint çâ s'fait que...* (in Canajan: 'howcum that...'). Cf. French **comment.*

CONÇARNE

One's place of employment. As in: *A travaille pour une grosse conçarne* (in Canajan: 'Shworks furra big comp'ny'). Cf. French **une forte société commerciale.*

COUNTING

It would be a mistake to think that joual speakers don't count. They do. It's just that they don't count like Francophones. Or at least not always.

To establish this scientifically a survey of the first ten cardinal numerals in joual was undertaken some years ago by the National Research Council with the aid of a grant from the Ford Foundation, no Canadian risk capital being available for the purpose. The results of this two-volume study are published here for the first time; the report itself has not yet been released by the NRC as they are still waiting for the French translation.

The study established beyond all peradventure that a fixed pattern of correspondence exists between joual and French counting; that it is present at all levels; and that it is invariable. Without going into the mathematical formulations involved (which are contained in a separate volume of computer printouts), the outline of this pattern may be stated with some concision. It is that for the first ten cardinal numerals joual and French terms alternate on a random basis.

This rule of random correspondence, as the NRC savants call it, may be exhibited in tabular form. In the schema which follows it should be noted that the left-hand column contains those cardinal numerals for which the same word is used by both joual speakers and Francophones; in the right-hand column are segregated those terms of purely joual origin.

TABLE 42. Rule of Random Correspondence In Joual Cardinal Numerals[1]

JOUAL/FRENCH	JOUAL
	In
Deux	
Trois	
	Quat'
	Cin'
	Siss
Sept	
	Witt
Neuf	
	Dziss

If another foundation grant is forthcoming the NRC hopes to carry the project further. At the present time almost nothing is known about the cardinal numerals beyond *dziss*, but it is certainly untrue that one cannot count beyond 10 in joual. Indeed, the present study (as yet unfunded) has already discerned the joual term for 100: it is *cint*, pronounced to rhyme with **vingt*. If only someone would put up the money, there is no reason why a start should not be made toward mapping the undiscovered country between *dziss* and *cint*, but it will take time.

[1]All figures are seasonally adjusted.

CREDDY TSISTS

See *Polly Tsick.*

RULE 5. Don't Stumble. Mumble.

As is well known, Standard French could not survive for two seconds without syllables. Moreover French syllables, unlike English syllables, must be spoken carefully and distinctly. No chewing, munching or swallowing is allowed.

For although Francophones speak very quickly — as anyone can attest who has ever tried to follow the dialogue in a French movie with one eye on the subtitles — they never mumble.

In fact, mumbling has been officially proscribed by the French Academy since 1639. Actually Louis XIII had established the Academy in 1635 but it took four years to find forty people who could speak French well enough to suit the king. When all armchairs had been filled, one of the first rules passed was against mumbling (*Art. 5: Contre le Marmottage*). This was done largely at the instigation of Cardinal Richelieu who didn't like the way some of the academicians were going about saying things under their breath. He reasoned that if everyone were obliged to speak up clearly, the risk of treason would be greatly reduced. Hence Art. 5 which staved off the French Revolution for 150 years.

This rule, although obviously passed for reasons of national

Sieur de Richardson

Sieur de Zolf

Sieur de Davis

Gerald de Regan

Sieur d'Onderwhere

Eugène d'Oofs

Le Duck d'Edinburr

The French Academy

security, was gradually adopted by every French pedagogue throughout the world, including my own teacher who used to tell her class very earnestly and distinctly: '*Il-faut-pro-non-cer-cha-que-syl-la-be-de-cha-que-mot.*' So rigorously has this rule been applied that true Frenchmen even pronounce the mute *e*.

Being young, we did our careless best to comply, quite unaware that joual Rule 5 (the numerical similarity to Art. 5 may be more than coincidental) dictated precisely the opposite course.

Rule 5 requires two quite separate and distinct verbal actions: (a) chewing or munching, and (b) swallowing, which taken together constitute (c) mumbling. The state of joual studies does not as yet permit us to examine these actions either separately or as part of an evolutionary process, but we can readily observe the results of the process, for example in the wholesale ingestion of vowels, one of the distinguishing marks of the people's language. These may be in terminal position, as when the older French forms **me*, **ce*, **de* and **le* become *m'*, *c'*, *d'* and *l'*. Thus: *y m'dzit* (in Canajan: 'He tole me'). Cf. French **il me dit*. But internal vowels slip just as easily down the gullet, as do consonants. Thus: *A l'a vu l'aut'jour* (in Canajan: 'She sawm thother day'); *S'ché pâ s'y est v'nu* (in Canajan: 'I dough no fee came'). Cf. French **Je ne sais pas s'il est venu*. Further examples will be found here and there in the text.

D

D'DINS

Inside, within. As in: *Prinds c'qu'y a d'dins.* (in Canajan: 'Take whut synod'). Cf. French **dedans*. Pronounce to rhyme with **vingt*.

DEUX NATIONS

Once upon a time there were two nations in Canada called *Angloterre*, or land of the Anglos, and *Joualande*, i.e., the country of the joual people.

Over the years their respective natives, the Anglos and the Jouals, lived together but apart in a state of mutual isolation and incomprehension known as Federalism.

Even though the modern trend in other countries was towards togetherness, Canajans continued to believe firmly in apartness. This is because the power of negative thinking was still strong in the land.

One example will suffice. In those days each of the two nations had its own separate currency, both being issued by the Bank of Canada. The currency intended for use in Angloterre was printed in English, while that for use in Joualande was printed in French. In this way the danger of fiscal pollution was reduced to a minimum.

When, however, in 1936 the government of the day announced its intention of issuing one set of banknotes in both languages, a storm of protest broke in parliament. The opposition argued strongly that such a proposal was contrary to the B.N.A. Act, that it deprived Canajans of the right to have a currency in the language of their choice, and that to do so could only result in the most disastrous consequences to Confederation.

Fortunately the debate took place in the depths of the Great Depression when, it was pointed out, nobody had any money anyway so that the question had no practical consequences. As a result bilingual currency was voted in without any apparent damage to the environment, but it was a close call.

DOMPER

To get rid of, jilt, abandon. As in: *Y a dompé sa blonde* (in Canajan: 'He dumped his broad'). Cf. French **plaquer.*

DOUÈTT

The finger. Pronounce 'dwet.' As in: *Alle a câssé le douètt* (in Canajan: 'Sh'broker finger'). Cf. French **doigt.* Other parts of the joual body may be noted in passing: e.g., *jveux,* the hair; *mosselles,* muscles; and so on.

D'PIS

Since (of time). Pronounce 'd'pee.' As in: *Allô! J't'vois pâ d'pis mardzi* (in Canajan: 'Hi! I dint seeya sints Chewsdy'). Sometimes also *d'pus*. Cf. French *depuis*.

DRET

Adjective signifying right, straight, direct, etc. Pronounce to rhyme with 'pet.' As in: *Va dret d'vant toé* (in Canajan: 'Gride ahead'); *dret comme une flèche* (in Canajan: 'strayed as an aero'). Cf. French *droit*.

DRETTE

The nominal form of *dret*. As in: *Alle était assise à ma drette* (in Canajan: 'She sadden my right').

E

EAU CANADÂ

Kay Beck has never had the same trouble about picking an anthem as the rest of the country since the most commonly accepted national song, *Eau Canadâ*, was (like Canada itself) French long before it was English. Most Anglos try not to think about things like that.

Acceptance of *Eau Canadâ* by Kay Beckers did not, however, come without a certain amount of trying. There were a number of earlier contenders, among them 'Remembering' (*Je me souviens*) and 'You've Forgotten Me' (*Tsu me souviens pâ*) which reflected, in turn, Kay Beck's attitude toward herself and to the rest of the country.

Introspective songs like these lacked the necessary verve for a true national anthem, however, and when Calixa Lavallée wrote the music for *Eau Canadâ* one night back in 1880, the piece became a smash hit next morning and has remained among the Top Ten ever since. It didn't do Lavallée himself much good, though, since, like so many Canadians before and after, he had to go to the United States to earn recognition and a living.

The words of *Eau Canadâ* were written down in French soon after by Sir Adolphe Routhier, the Chief Justice of Kay Beck (to make them legal) and then written down all over again in English by the Hon. R. Stanley Weir, a judge of the Exchequer Court (in a dissenting opinion). As history makes clear, the English and French have never been able to agree about anything in Canada, and the words of *Eau Canadâ* are no exception.

As far as poetry is concerned, there is little to choose between the two versions, which only goes to show what judges can do if you give them enough rope. Hence the movement to abolish capital punishment.

One popular version of the song runs practically as follows:

Eau Canadâ! O air aumône n'a t'y vlan de!
Troupe âtre iode l'eux vine hale saille sonne ce qu'amende.
Ouïsse clos un quartz oui scyte y rase
Zut roux norse tronc gant frit;
Anse tende oncques arde, Eau Canadâ,
Ouïsse tende oncques arde fort scie.
[Corps eusse]
Eau Canadâ! clore yeuse Indes frit!
Ouïsse tende oncques arde, ouïsse tende oncques arde fort scie.
Eau Canadâ, ouïsse tende oncques arde fort scie!

It may be recalled that a parliamentary committee, unhappy about the repetitiveness of the last five lines (an old failing of judges), rewrote them to read somewhat like this:

Freux me phare Andes ouaille d'Eau Canadâ
Ouïsse tende oncques arde fort scie.
[Corps eusse]
Gode qui porc l'âne de clore yeuse Indes frit!
Eau Canadâ, ouïsse tende oncques arde fort scie.
Eau Canadâ, ouïsse tende oncques arde fort scie!

The Revised Version is not yet official, however, and is rarely heard either on or off Parliament Hill.

EJ'

What happens to *je* when you apply Rule 19, *q.v.*

EKSÉTÉRA

Et cetera (in Canajan: 'essettra').

EKSIPRÈS, par

Intentionally. As in: *Y l'a fait par eksiprès* (in Canajan: 'He diddid on purps'). Cf. French **Il l'a fait exprès*.

EL'

Le seen through the looking-glass of Rule 19, *q.v.*

'Ouïsse tende oncques arde fort scie.'

ENTÉKA

Common joual adverb and conjunction signifying in any case, at any rate (in Canajan: 'anyways'). Cf. French *en tout cas*.

ESSE

East. Pronounce to rhyme with 'mess.' As in: *l'vint d'esse* (in Canajan: 'theest wind'). Cf. French *est*.

ÉTÂTS, LES

The U.S.A. Pronounce somewhat like 'lazy taw' (in Canajan: 'The Hugh Ess,' 'The Knighted States'). Cf. French *Les États Unis.*

ÉTRE

The auxilliary verb 'to be.' Pronounce the first syllable like 'eye.' See *Chus.*

F

FAIR SHARE, MARIE MADELEINE DE

An early joual heroine, Madeleine de Fair Share won renown as an Indian fighter in the days before that sort of thing was un-Canajan.

From when she was a little girl Mad couldn't stop fighting Indians. It just got to her. The ones they mostly had trouble with were the Irk Wah. Every time Mad saw one she used to let fly with whatever was at hand — a doll, a carrot, a dishpan, etc. — and then she would add another notch to her little broom handle.

It all started at their seigniory on the Sen Lornz River when, at the tender age of twelve, Mad watched her mother stand off a band of marauding Irk Wah for two days (her father had gone to pick up the mail which was notoriously slow in those days).

Not two years later Mad was called on to do the same thing, only this time both her parents were away taking part in a demonstration for day-care centres and she had been left in charge of a younger brother and sister. Although scarcely fourteen, Mad, without a moment's hesitation, gathered a few old women and children into the fort and kept them all blazing away with dolls, carrots, dishpans, etc., for eight days until the army (which was also notoriously slow in those days) arrived from Mont Ray-all.

When the King's soldiers lifted the siege and reported the Irk Wah body count to the Governor, Mad was granted a Royal Pension.

As time went on, Mad acquired a husband, Pierre, and five children, but it wasn't easy. On one occasion she saved her husband's life when he was attacked by an Irk Wah to whom Pierre had made an ethnic remark. In later life she stopped fighting Irk Wahs and started fighting with her neighbours, but by then her place in history was secure.

Her story illustrates the basic mistake which the early French Canajans made by shutting themselves up in forts and stockades while allowing the Irk Wah to run at large. This meant that every time a settler ventured forth to pick a handful of peas or go bushing, he ran the risk of bumping into an Irk Wah, which made it very inconvenient to complete his mission.

The Anglos, on the other hand, devised a much better system in the part of the country which they had liberated by shutting their Indians up in large pens called reservations, while they themselves could move about quite freely. That way it was the Indians who got into trouble whenever they ventured forth.

In any case, after the great peace of 1701, there weren't all that many Irk Wah left, so the French Canajans switched to fighting Anglos who were becoming more plentiful (see *Mont Kam*). Unfortunately it took the French Canajans a long time to figure out where they had gone wrong, and by that time the eighteenth century was half over and it was too late.

FARME-TOÉ

A short but not overly hostile invitation to stop talking (in Canajan: 'Ah, shuddup!'). The stronger expression is *Ta yeule!* (in Canajan: 'Shutcher trap!' which should not be used in the drawing-room). Cf. French *taisez-vous*.

FÉKE

Anything fraudulent. As in: *çâ c't'un féke* (in Canajan: 'Sa phoney'). Cf. French *chose truquée*. The verbal form is *féker*, as in: *A féke* (in Canajan: 'Sheez faken'). Cf. French *truquer*.

FÉVÉRIER

Second month in the joual calendar, sometimes also *feuvrier* (in Canajan: 'Febboo wary'). Cf. French *février*. Other joual months to remember are *avri* (cf. French *avril*); *jun*, pronounced with the nasal sound of *un* (cf. French *juin*); and *août*, pronounced 'a-oo' with two syllables.

FLAILLER

To decamp, to leave in a great hurry. Pronounce to rhyme with 'Fly, eh?' As in: *Flaille-toé, v'là les boeufs!* (in Canajan: 'Bead it, the fuzz!'). Cf. French *filer*.

FONNE

Fun, amusement. As in: *Y trouve çâ ben l'fonne* (in Canajan: 'Slodda fun'). Similarly: *A l'a fait pour l'fonne* (in Canajan: 'Sh'diddit jisfer fun'). Cf. French *pour rire*. Also appears in the adjectival form *fonné*. Cf. French *amusant*, *drôle*.

FRÈTE

Cold. Pronounce like 'fret.' As in: *Y fait frète à matin* (in Canajan: 'Scold smorning'). Cf. French *froid*.

FRONT KNACK

The Governor of Nooph Rance was usually a member of the nobility or someone's relative, chosen by the King because he needed money and so would be loyal. He was assisted by the Intendant who kept (and sometimes cooked) the books. Together they looked after the King's interests in peace and war, which was a full-time job since everything belonged to the King in those

days. The Bishop's job was to justify this arrangement to the habitants who did all the work.

These three men — Governor, Intendant and Bishop — ruled Nooph Rance, thus illustrating the Old Bourbon motto: 'Everthing for the King and God help the people.'

Front Knack, the greatest of the French governors, won early renown as a fighter. He fought the Briddish; he fought the Irk Wah. And when they were pacified he fought the Intendant and the Bishop. In between times he fought the furt raiders. In fact, he made such a nuisance of himself, what with all his fighting, that the King had to recall him. The only person he didn't fight with was his wife.

But his successors proved to be so peace-loving that in a few years the Irk Wah were shooting up the main street of Lachine and Front Knack had to be brought back to re-pacify them. He did this with such success that before the end of his second term there were very few Irk Wah around. Then he died in bed.

FURT RAID, the

No account of the early days of Nooph Rance would be complete without some discussion of the Furt Raid which, by progressively eliminating most fur-bearing animals, contributed greatly to the building of Canada.

As we have seen, the French King kept an eye on the little colony by sending three men to oversee it. The Intendant kept an eye on men's pocketbooks. The Bishop kept an eye on men's souls. And the Governor kept an eye on the Intendant and the Bishop. With so many eyes around, it was hard for most ordinary people to make an honest living.

Partly for this reason the Furt Raid grew up, first in a small way by some early settler relieving a stray Irk Wah of his pelt, and later on in a more organized fashion. The French tried to extend their traplines westward but found themselves squeezed between the Hudson's Bay Company posts to the north and the American traders to the south. As a result much rivalry ensued and often practical solutions had to be found. Thus competition for the lucrative sea-otter trade on the Pacific coast ended when there weren't any more sea-otters. But not all problems could be solved so easily. Sometimes it was necessary to impose political and military solutions. So when Wolf defeated Mont Kam at Kay Beck, the Americans moved in and ran the Furt Raid since there was at that time no screening agency to prevent American takeovers. At the same time, by a series of treaties, Britain and the United States agreed to exclude Canadian traders from U.S. territory, thus establishing the general commercial pattern between the two countries which has prevailed to this day.

G

GANG

A group or crowd. Sometimes written *gagne* but pronounced 'gang.' As in: *une gang d'amis*, a bunch of friends; *toute la gang*, the whole crowd. Cf. French **troupe*.

GARAOUGE

Pronounce 'ga-row-ge,' the middle syllable to rhyme with the Yankee 'naow.' Place where one stores or repairs the joual *châr*, *q.v.* (in Canajan: 'gradge' or 'grodge').

GENTSI

Gentle, nice. As in the old football song: *'Alouette, gentsi Alouette...'* Cf. French **gentil*.

GOUVARNEMAGNE

Body of persons governing the province or country. The last syllable is pronounced to rhyme with 'gang.' As in: *Y perle toujous conte le gouvarnemagne* (in Canajan: 'Heez olleys talkin gainst the gummint'). Cf. French **gouvernement*.

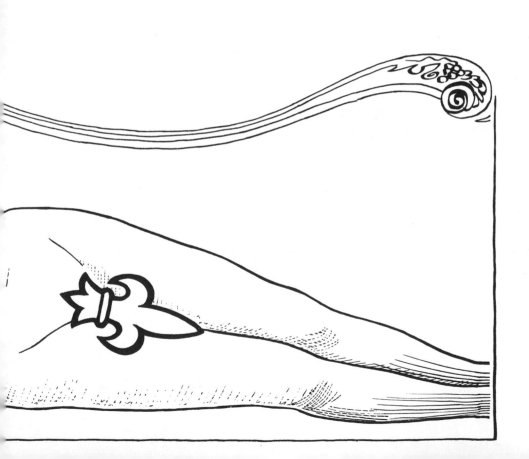

RULE 9. All Joual Verbs Are Irregular.

Former students of French will recall the bad time they had with verbs. First there were all those conjugations of regular verbs to be memorized. Then some otherwise regular verbs had orthographical peculiarities. Verbs of this class would be irregular if they dared, but lacked the courage to go all the way. Finally there were the irregular verbs themselves, rank upon serried rank, formidable battalions which cowed even the stoutest memory.

The infighting was ruthless. All those regular endings to be learned. Then the exceptions. Then the exceptions to the exceptions. Learning French verbs was a traumatic battle from which few Anglos ever emerged unscathed.

Joual eliminates all this carnage with the simple rule enunciated above. Since all joual verbs are irregular there is no need to go through the lacerating struggle which we have been considering. No need to learn first the regular verbs and then all the exceptions. In joual *every* verb is an exception, which instantly cuts the learning process in half. And since we are only concerned with varying degrees of irregularity, each verb is as good as its neighbour. In this way all problems are quickly eliminated. A joual speaker simply talks the way his mother did and everybody understands everybody else.

H

HÉ?

Anglosaxophones may boast their famous four-letter words, but Canada's great little two-letter word 'eh?' tops them all when it comes to ubiquity. Neither provincial boundaries nor the Property and Civil Rights section of the B.N.A. Act has been able to stop the relentless spread of 'eh?' into every corner of the country.

The reason is simple. All-purpose, heavy-duty 'eh?' soon won acceptance everywhere, Kay Beck and Far Northern areas included, nor could the result have been otherwise. The fact remains that there is just no substitute for 'eh?' and Canajans of every stripe have wisely refrained from trying to find one.

Even Kay Beck's determination to run her own dining-room in her own way (*maîtres d'hôtel chez nous*) proved to be no match for the mighty monosyllable, and regardless of who was in power (see *Polly Tsick*) or whether the *langue de travail* was Canajan or joual (see *Introduction*) in no time at all 'eh?' was in every mouth.

It is, of course, an inflexible rule of Kay Beck life that everthing must be done the opposite way around from the rest of the country. To comply with this rule, the spelling of 'eh?' had to be reversed; hence the joual form *hé?* (the initial *h* may be aspirated or not according to individual taste, although most people find that it tastes better unaspirated).

Broadly speaking, *hé?* may be used in every life-situation where Canajan 'eh?' is called for. For all practical purposes the two words are interchangeable.

In order to achieve supremacy in Kay Beck, *hé?* had first to meet and vanquish the Standard French **hein?* While the contest between *hé?* and **hein?* belongs more properly to the field of socio-linguistics with overtones of Structuralism, a brief account may be given here since our French Canajan scholiasts have not seen fit to record it. This is typical of their attitude toward joual (see *Personal Note*).

*Hein? started off badly since, besides looking implausible, it has a nasal and querulous sound. Then it ran foul of certain nationalists of the Canon Groulx school who objected to having the thought-forms of a foreign culture imposed upon them. After all, they argued, what is common currency on the Boulevard St. Germain sounds counterfeit along *Ste. Katrinne esse.*

A more serious fault was that **hein?* lacked the signalling or attention-getting quality of *hé?* Its range was smaller, being confined basically to interrogation and astonishment. Finally, in an argument which was frankly *ad populum*, the government of the day urged that adoption of the standard Canajan term 'eh?' would mark a great step forward for co-operative federalism. That turned the tide and, with the orthographical change noted above, *hé?* it has been ever since.

HOT WATERR

Main thoroughfare in Mont Ray-all *wesse*. Also a Métro station. Aspirate initial *h* lightly or not at all and place stress on last syllable.

Mont Ray-all is the only Canajan city to have a subway system in technicolour and wall-to-wall muzak, which makes it second to none in underground society. This wasn't easy as the trains had first to be bent to go around the mountain. Then the passengers had to be bent to go into the trains.

I

ICITTE

Here, in this place. As in: *V'nez icitte* (in Canajan: 'C'mere').
Icitte is apparently in breach of Rule 1, enunciated above, since it
looks longer and not shorter than the Standard French term **ici*;
something seems to have been added rather than subtracted.
However, it is a bad rule which has no exceptions, and Rule 1,
while a pretty bad rule, is not all that bad. In any event, Rule
17, *q.v.*, was enacted to take care of all cases not covered by Rule 1.

'IEN

A good example of joual apheresis (see Rule 1). *'Ien* is the
equivalent of Canajan 'nuthin' (itself a good example of Canajan
apocope). Cf. French **rien*.

ITOU

In addition, besides. As in: *moé itou* (in Canajan: 'meatoo'). Cf.
French **aussi*.

IYOÙ

Where. The long form of French **où*. See Rule 17.

J

JOUAL

The people's language of Kay Beck. The word joual is said to derive from the popular pronunciation of *cheval*, i.e., horse, although at first glance it is not clear what a horse has to do with the folk speech of French Canada. We are little wiser at second glance if we look at the dictionary definition of horse: a solid-hoofed quadruped with long mane and tail, ridden and used as a beast of burden. Any connection seems remote since, so far as we are aware, no Kay Beckers are quadrupeds and even fewer have manes and tails.

JOUALANDE

See *Deux Nations*.

JUSSE

Just, just enough. As in: *Nous sommes à jusse de lait* (in Canajan: 'We've jiss enough melk').

JVEUX

The hair. See *Douètt*. Do not confuse with *j'veux* (in Canajan: 'I wanna'). The apostrophe makes all the difference. Cf. French *cheveux*.

K

KETCHOPPE

Expression of reassurance. As in: *L'affaire est ketchoppe* (in Canajan: 'Sin the bag'). Cf. French *C'est dans le sac*.

L

LA TSUQUE

Town on the St. Mauriss River, northwest of Kay Beck City.

LÉ

It. As in *dites-lé* (in Canajan: 'sayt'); *faites-lé* (in Canajan: 'doot'). Pronounce like 'lay.'

LETTE

Letter. As in: *Mette une lette à la posse* (in Canajan: 'Pudda lerr in the mail'). Cf. French *lettre*.

LI

Past participle of *lire*, 'to read.' Pronounce 'lee.' As in: *J'ai li çâ su' les papiers* (in Canajan: 'I sot n'tha paper'). Cf. French *J'ai lu ça dans les journaux.*

LINDZI

The second day of the week. Pronounce the first syllable with the nasal sound of *vingt*. The days of the joual week, in sucessive order, are as follows: *dzimanche, lindzi, mardzi, méquerdzi,*

judzi, venderdzi and *sémdzi*. The comparable Canajan days are:
Sundy, Mundy, Chewsdy, Wensdy, Thursdy, Fridy and Sarrdy.

RULE 12. In Case Of Doubt, The Use Of An English Word Is Always Correct And Will Be Perfectly Understood.

One of the glories of English is the way in which many languages
of the world have been welcomed into her bed — German
(*chain-smoker*), Italian (*flu*), Arabic (*alcohol*), Indian (*loot*),
Chinese (*tea*), Polynesian (*tattoo*) — all have submitted to her
maternal embrace and their offspring proudly bear the mother's
name.

Not so the stately French language, however, which has
always been old-maidish about permitting foreigners to take
liberties under the bedclothes. Most have been chased out with
some indignation, and the few that remain — *le higlif, le
weekend, le smoking, le drugstore* — feel awkward and insecure
in the knowledge that *la belle France* will always look on them as
outside children.

By contrast, joual has lived common law with Canajan for so
long that the union is sanctified by the rule enunciated above,
and their lusty brood tumbles about on the kitchen floor without

any inhibitions whatsoever. Examples will be found throughout the text, but by way of illustration a short list is appended:

joual	Canajan	French
avrège	avridge	*moyenne
béloné	bloney	*mortadelle
bommer	bum round	*flâner
bougrer l' camp	bug roff	*foutre le camp
caméra	camra	*appareil (photographique)
gradzuation	gradjayshn	*collation des grades
légal	lea gull	*juridique
mutsuel	mewtch'll	*commun
opératriss	operader	*téléphoniste
passé dû	pass doo	*échu
tsube	choob	*lampe

As appears from the above, whenever Rule 12 sanctions the use of an English word, it must be pronounced *à la jouale*. Otherwise the Rule would be neocolonialist, and also in violation of the Brish North America Act.

M

MAN

The familiar term for one's female parent, viz., Mom. Remember to pronounce with the nasal sound of *vingt* and not that of *enfant*.

    Man is commonly used when calling out to attract attention. In normal conversational usage, however, the preferred term is *moman*.

MARCI

Expression of gratitude, sometimes accompanied by the intensive *ben*. As in: *marci ben* (in Canajan: 'Thang slot'). Cf. French **merci bien*.

MÉRE

One's female parent. Pronounce somewhere between 'mare' and 'mire.' Cf. *man*.

    In direct speech one should never apply the possessive adjective *ma* to one's mother, but always the third person *sa*. Thus: *'Coute sa mére* (in Canajan: 'Lissen, ma').

    Mére may also be used when speaking to a husband about his spouse. As in: *'Allô, Jacques! C'mint est la mére?'* (in Canajan: 'Hi, Jack! Howza wife?').

    For one's male parent see *pére*.

MOÉ

Me, the objective case of I. Pronounced to rhyme more or less with 'gway.'

    Moé, along with its companion *toé*, pronounced 'tway,' is one of those basic indicators which may be used to distinguish a Kay Becker from a Francophone. Only schoolteachers and people who want you to think that they have come up in the world would attempt the Standard French forms *moi* and *toi*.

Moé and *toé* are, of course, the objective cases of 'I' and 'thou,' and care must be taken to distinguish them from the nominative forms. In view of the difficulty which some Anglos experience with joual personal pronouns, the first two will now be considered briefly.

The first person singular nominative form is *j'*, as in: *J'comprinds 'ien* (in Canajan: 'I doan geddit'). The objective form, as noted above, is *moé*, as in: *'Qui c'est qui est lâ?' 'C'est moé'* (in Canajan: 'Hoozair?' 'Smee').

The second person singular nominative form is *tsu*, as in: *Comprinds-tsu pâ?* (in Canajan: 'Doancha unnerstand?'). The objective form, as noted above, is *toé*, as in: *C'est toé?* (in Canajan: 'Zachoo?'). For the third person pronouns see *A* and *Y*.

The most celebrated *moé* of history was Louis XIV's *'L'État c'est Moé.'*

MOE DZEE

When the entire joual vocabulary of Mont Ray-all was run through a computer recently, the expression which occurred with the highest frequency was found to be *moe dzee*.

As an imprecation the connection with French *maudit* is

almost discernible, but this aspect of the matter need not detain us here. Rather we will consider *Moe Dzee* in its eponymous sense.

As the true patron saint of Kay Beck, Moe should be distinguished from Jean Bateese, the paper or official patron saint, who has a day specially reserved for him in the Calendar but is otherwise largely ignored by the devout. Moe's observances, on the other hand, are confined to no one day or occasion. His name is taken in vain constantly and at the slightest provocation by all joual speakers.

Little is known of Moe's origins. Some have posited that he is part of an Old Testament thread which runs through Kay Beck's story (cf. the Plains of Abraham) and that French Canajans are the lost tribes of Israel, but this story lacks the weight of scholarly approval. Indeed, hagiographers have largely disregarded Moe's existence, much as teachers have treated joual with studied neglect (see *Introduction*) as though it were something which would go away if only one ignored it long enough. Other commentators have claimed to find in *Moe Dzee* a western transliteration of Mao Tse, which would locate his origins in Sinology rather than Sinai.

But like all folk saints, *Moe Dzee* is far too clever and tenacious to be dislodged by any paper saint, just as joual itself will never be displaced by any mere official language. One may confidently predict that both of them will be around for a long time to come, no matter who's in charge.

MON DOU

A mild oath. See *Bon Yeu*.

MONT KAM, LOOIE DE

If the Battle of Waterloo was won on the playing fields of Eton, Nooph Rance was lost on the hockey rinks of Kay Beck. The latter fact is less well-known than the former because joual history has largely been written by Anglos. Thus we have been led to believe all along that Jimmy Wolf and his Redcoats beat Looie Mont Kam and his Canadziens in fair combat. As usual, however, truth is stranger than faction.

What happened is that the Stanley Cup finals of that fateful year were definitely not on the level.

As September 13, 1759 approached, Mont Kam's team had already made a clean sweep of the playoffs, beating the Anglos four straight at Oswego, Ticonderoga, Fort William Henry and Montmorency. Now he saw his chance to get around the finals and clinch the Cup with a sudden-death game.

Already in his mind's eye Looie could see the headlines in next day's *Quebec Gazette*: 'Habs Blank Anglos. Riot at Forum.' But when his arch-enemy, Vode Roy, pointed out to him that the *Gazette* wasn't founded until 1764, he should have seen that his dreams were running far ahead of reality.

In fact, his team was tired and poorly-equipped. There was much dissension between the French regulars and the joual militia who were very irregular. They kept getting their boots mixed up and arguing over each other's pronunciation, about which the French tended to be very superior. In addition the Intendant, Bigot, besides being a crook was very prejudiced against the French Canajans (*Quel bigot!* was a commonly-heard complaint) and there was much hard feeling about the pay scales. The French were paid in *louis d'or* while the Canadziens got nickels and dimes, which was very bad for morale.

Worst of all, the British naval blockade of Kay Beck prevented Mont Kam from bringing in imports to bolster his team, while Wolf, thanks to mastery of the seas and the infamous farm system, was able to ship in fresh players at will.

This was the situation when the Governor, Vode Roy, dropped the opening puck. The constant bickering between Vode Roy and Mont Kam was, of course, notorious and it will come as no surprise to learn that Vode Roy threw the game before it started by giving the Anglo coach a copy of all the Habs' secret signals. As well he favoured Wolf immediately after the face-off by handing out game penalties to all the joual players. This left Mont Kam with nothing but Frenchmen who played Canajan hockey like a Spanish cow.

The Habs made a half-hearted attempt to mount a power play, but before you could say: 'He shoots! He scores!' a veritable orgy of infractions broke out all over the place: hooking, tripping, holding, high-sticking, boarding. In a twinkling the rule book was torn to shreds and the whistles were drowned in a cloud of boos and programs.

Cries of *'A bas les Anglos!'* and *'L'arbitre est un robber!'* rang out when the referee tried to call the play for icing but by then everybody was offside, and in the general mayhem which followed the Habs fell back first to their own blue line, and then to their dee fence of zone. The Canajan team rallied briefly when both the players' bench and the penalty box emptied onto the rink, and even the Habs' goalie was pulled out of the net, but by then it was too late. While Mont Kam was still arguing with the referee, the Anglos cleared the ice, stowed away the nets, pocketed the puck and declared the game over.

It is true that before play started, Mont Kam had plans to fight on at the Ohio or the Mississippi if he lost at Kay Beck, but this would have been minor-league stuff. To have won later in the boondocks would have convinced nobody. The blunt fact was that the Habs had blown the big one. By an Anglo trick, to be sure, but without instant replay this could not be verified, and so the verdict of history went against Mont Kam.

MONT RAY-ALL

The largest English-speaking French city in the world. The first syllable is nasalized to rhyme with *mon, ton* or *con*.

Mont Ray-all was found (although not founded) in 1535 by Jock Car Chay, *q.v.*, who according to the book was welcomed by 1000 native people with bonfires and feasting. This was their first mistake. Car Chay also discovered Mount Royal, which was really not very difficult since it is 759 feet high and hard to miss particularly before the tall buildings went up.

Mont Ray-all was founded (but not found) in 1642 by Maisonneuve who changed the name from Hochelaga which people said was too ethnic. At the first Mass (it took some time to build a church because bingo had not yet been invented), Pére Vimont uttered the famous words: 'What you see is only a grain of mustard seed … but it must be that God has great designs for it.' This proved to be indeed a prophetic remark. While it is not clear which of the 245 species of mustard found in Canada the good father had in mind, the manufacture of this essential condiment has grown to match a massive hot-dog and hamburger industry whose dimensions could scarcely have been anticipated in 1642.

MOSSELLES

Muscles. See *Douètt*. Cf. French **muscles*.

N

NEIN

A negative response. Pronounce with the nasal sound of (and to rhyme with) *vingt*. Do not confuse with German *nein*, although the two words may be cognate. Thus: *'Tsu veux pâ v'nir?' 'Nein!'* (in Canajan: 'Ya dough wanna come?' 'Nah!'). Cf. French *non*.

NEU

A part of the verbal phrase *y a 'ien d'neu* (in Canajan: 'znuthin noo'). Cf. French *il n'y a rien de nouveau*.

NN

Joual pronoun signifying 'some' or 'any.' As in: *A nn a* (in Canajan: 'Sheeze gotsum'). Cf. French *elle en a*.

NOT'

Attentive readers will recall that joual Rule 1, subsection 3, *q.v.*, calls for the extensive use of apocope, or giving the chop to the rear end.

Examples of posterior abscission abound, but here it will suffice to note the first and second person plural forms of the possessive adjective (cf. in the standard language the archaic or presumed forms *notre* and *votre*). Joual speakers by the application of Rule 1 (3) save time and energy by utilizing the forms *not'* and *vot'* respectively, as in: *not' pére* (in Canajan: 'are father'); *vot' tchomme* (in Canajan: 'yer buddy').

Joual has a distinct edge over Canajan in that instances of reduplicated avulsion are not uncommon. Thus: *Où c'est que not' liv'* (in Canajan: 'Wears are book?'). Cf. French *Où est notre livre*.

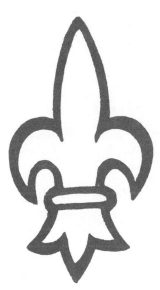

O

OCULISSE

A specialist in eye diseases. Cf. French *oculiste*, Other distinctive joual professions or occupations include *archétèque* (in Canajan: 'artiteck'), cf. French *architecte*; *artsisse* (in Canajan: 'ardist'), cf. French *artiste*; and *dentsisse* (in Canajan: 'dennis'), cf. French *dentiste*.

O.K. D'ABOWER

Expression of approval for something done by someone else (in Canajan: 'saul write'). Cf. French *ça va comme ça*.

ORDER

To order (something). Pronounce 'or day.' As in: *As-tsu ordé une draffe?* (in Canajan: 'Djorder a draft?'). Cf. French *As-tu commandé un demi?*

OUAI

The affirmative particle 'yes.' Pronounce somewhere between 'whey' and 'why.' There is no one Canajan equivalent for the joual *ouai*. Instead a range of alternatives is available: yeh, ya, yuh, yaw, yup, etc. As usual joual demonstrates its admirable concision. Cf. French *oui*.

OUESSE

West. Pronounce 'wess.' As in: *l'vint d'ouesse* (in Canajan: 'the wesswind'). Cf. French *ouest*.

OUJORD'HUI

The day after yesterday and before tomorrow (in Canajan: 't'day'). Cf. French *aujourd'hui*.

RULE 17. If You Can't Make It Shorter, Make It Longer.

In language, as in life, every rule has its opposite rule which is of equal force and effect. This means that if you are caught out on any given rule, you can always invoke another one. Some lawyers have built a very lucrative career on this simple principle.

An unthinking person might conclude that rules of this kind cancel each other out, but this is not so. The fact is that they are mutually supportive. Indeed, sometimes a countervailing rule has to be enacted to prop up an earlier one which shows signs of losing its grip.

Thus, when the oldest rule in the book, Rule 1, *q.v.*, was found to be inadequate to cover all cases, Rule 17 was enunciated in substantially the form which appears above. Did this nullify Rule 1? Not at all. It just doubled the possibilities.

This principle is well illustrated by the evolution of the presumed French term *où*, meaning 'where.' Obviously such a word affords little scope for the application of Rule 1: it is already so short that the possibility of further abridgment is severely limited. Does a joual speaker then remain content with *ou? Certainly not. He simply invokes Rule 17. Since *oǔ cannot be shortened it must be lengthened. Nothing could be simpler.

Linguists have discerned two modes of implementing Rule 17. The primitive approach is to tack on a few extra phonemes, a crude but perfectly effective method. In this way *oǔ has become *iyoǔ*, as in: *Iyoǔ que t'es allé?* (in Canajan: 'Wearja go?').

But joual can achieve more impressive effects by syntactic build-up. Thus from *oǔ has been derived *oǔ que* which means the same thing but sounds much better. Should this be insufficient, more complicated syntactical paradigms are available to the joual speaker. Consider, for example, the following variations on the simple theme *Oǔ vas-tu?*, i.e., 'Where are you going?':

> *Oǔ que tsu vâs?*
> *Oǔ ce que tsu vâs?*
> *Oǔ c'est que tsu vâs?*
> *Oǔ que c'est que tsu vâs?*

As against all this richness Canajan can only offer the unadorned 'Wear'ya goyne?'

P

PÂ

No, not. Pronounce with a vowel sound located somewhere
between that of 'paw' and the first syllable of 'porridge.' Joual *pâ*
carries so strong a negative charge that the standard *ne* is
completely redundant and must be omitted. Thus French **ne ...
pas* is in joual simply *pâ*. As in: *Tsu l'vois pâ?* (in Canajan:
'Dontcha seam?'). Cf. French **Tu ne le vois pas?*

PARTSI KAY BECKWAH

See *Polly Tsick*.

PASSE QUE

For the reason that, since. As in: *A veut pâ v'nir passe que chus icitte* (in Canajan: 'Shwon't come becuz I mere'). Cf. French *parce que*.

PÉPÉ

The Kay Beck Provincial Police. As in: *'Flaille-toé! La Pépé!'* (in Canajan: 'Beadit! The Per Vinshuls!').

PÉRE

One's male parent. Pronounce somewhere between 'pare' and 'pyre.'

Following the example of *mére*, one addresses one's father formally by means of the possessive adjective *son* rather than *mon*, as in: *Bonjour, son pére* (where *bonjour* means 'goodbye').

On less formal occasions the word *pepa* may be used to approximate 'pop' or 'dad.' *Pépé*, on the other hand, means 'grand-dad.'

PÉTAQUES

Edible tubers of a plant much cultivated in Kay Beck. As in: *pétaques mâchées* (in Canajan: 'mash bodaydoes'). Cf. French *patates, pommes de terre*.

PIASSES

Dollars, bucks. As in: *Y ganne cint piasses par s'maine* (in Canajan: 'He gets a hunnerd bucksa week'). Cf. French *piastres*.

PINOTTE

Peanut. Cf. French *cacahuète*.

PIS

Joual adverb signifying then, after that. Pronounce like 'pee.' As in: *et pis quoi?* (in Canajan: 'so what?'); *pis a est partsi* (in Canajan: 'nthen shleft'). *Pis* may also be used conjunctively, as in: *On est bons amis, lui pis moé* (in Canajan: 'We're good friends, him'n me'). Do not confuse with *pus*, *q.v.* Cf. French *puis*.

POLLY TSICK, LA

La polly tsick has basically the same function in Kay Beck as paul ticks does in the Anglo parts of the country. That is to say, it is a game played with high seriousness by its respective teams, and largely ignored by the public except during the playoffs which occur every four years.

Although a fairly consistent game plan is followed

throughout Anglo Canada, Kay Beck has never been a province like the others, *hé?* As an example of the difference we may consider briefly the career of the late Morris Dupe Lessee, familiarly called *le chef* by his followers because he always had something cooking.

Dupe Lessee goes back to an era in Kay Beck when *la polly tsick* was much more free and easy than at present. In those days the province operated on the delivery system, which went somewhat as follows. Firstly the Church delivered the rural vote. Next a few big city bosses like Montreal's Mayor Who'd delivered the urban vote. The per vinshul vote was then delivered to Dupe Lessee, while at the fed rull level La Point delivered the whole thing to Oddawa. As with most commercial transactions, all deliveries were C.O.D.

This kind of system operated well enough for many years until, in the early 1960's, came the quiet revelation that Kay Beck could go it alone (*Maîtres chez nous*) if only it switched from cash to credit. This simple formula transformed French Canajan society overnight. Instead of the blank cheque which other provinces had accused it of demanding from Oddawa, Kay Beck got a credit card, thereby enabling it to live far beyond its means just like everybody else.

At one stroke the old cash-and-carry-on system of Dupe

Lessee was swept away. Now for the first time French Canajans could have whatever they wanted without delivering anything. It was indeed the end of an era.

Anglo Canada was slow to catch on at first, being preoccupied as usual with substance rather than form. The Bye and Bye Commission had proceeded on the assumption that Canada was a partnership of two found-in races. From this premise it was but a step for some to assert that there were not merely two races but two nations. The Conserve Tuvs went on at great length with their doo nass yawns theory, but after a while the thing became boring and was dropped at the next election, along with the Conserve Tuvs.

Somehow this all got confused in people's minds with the question of whether Canada was a mosaic or a melting-pot; that is, whether its component parts remained bits and pieces or became a pudding. The Lib Rulls, following the tradition of William Lyin Mackenzie King, plumped for form rather than substance ('doo nass yawns if necessary, but not necessarily doo nass yawns'). As a result of this adherence to their old principles, they swept Kay Beck at the next election and were returned triumphantly to Oddawa with a minority government. The Endy Pee made no headway at all, since in those days Kay Beck was too poor to afford socialism, even on credit.

In fact, the great switch to credit brought a new plitti cull grouping to the fore. The quiet revulsion over lack of cash had turned many French Canajans off. Now they rallied to the banner of the Creddy Tsists, a joual version of the old Soak Reds. This group believed that they could have the best of both economic systems by issuing cash to the public on credit. If the resultant cash were then used to pay off the credit, more credit could then be made available on the strength of which more cash could be issued with which to pay off the new credit, and then further credit could be extended which ...Clearly the possibilities were endless.

While the Anglos were still trying to figure that one out, another group was working toward a quiet revocation of Confederation on the principle that the whole is less than some of its parts. For many years a few Kay Beckers had dreamed of taking their piece of the Sen Lornz River and starting a new country someplace else. When it was pointed out that the river was connected at both ends to other people's water, they reluctantly agreed to settle for a new country where they were. Such were the beginnings of the seppra tsiste movement.

For a long time most people felt that a new country was a luxury which Kay Beckers could never afford. But the quiet cash-credit revaluation of the sixties changed all that. People soon realized that it was no longer necessary to save up for things as they used to do in the old days. Now there was no reason why they couldn't be independent on somebody else's money. The only question was, whose?

With that quiet realization the Partsi Kay Beckwah was born, dedicated to the proposition that either Kay Beck must leave Canada or Canada must leave Kay Beck. Now the group had a name and an aim. The name was later abbreviated to *Paye Cul*, in memory of all the years when Kay Beck had to pay through the nose for everything.

POSSE

The mail. See *Lette*. Cf. French **poste*.

PUS

Adverb signifying more, anymore. Pronounce with the unpronounceable French *u* sound, half-way between 'poo' and 'pee.' As in: *Y veut pus* (in Canajan: 'He dough want nomore'); *moé non pus* (in Canajan: 'me neither'). Also to mark the comparative, as in: *pus meilleur* (in Canajan: 'bedder'). Do not confuse with *pis, q.v.* Cf. French **plus*.

Q

QUÂRT

Fifteen minutes. Pronounce somewhere between 'core' and
'cower.' As in: *Y est witt heures moins quârt* (in Canajan:
'Squorda aid'). A few other joual times of day may be noted:
onze heures et dziss (in Canajan: 'tempus leven'). Also *siss heures
et d'mie* (in Canajan: 'happis six').

QUÉ'QU'CHOSE

Equivalent to Canajan 'sumpm'. As in: *'Coute, son pére, j'ai
qué'qu'chose à t'dzire* (in Canajan: 'Lissen, Dad, I got sumpm ta
tellya'). Cf. French *quelque chose*.

QUÉ'QU'PART

Equivalent to Canajan 'summers.' As in: *J'l'ai vu qué'qu'part* (in
Canajan: 'I sawm summers'). Cf. French *quelque part*.

QUOUÉ

What. Pronounce somewhere between 'kway' and 'kwy.' As in:
Y a pâ de quoué à manger (in Canajan: 'He has'n whut teat').
Cf. French *Il n'a pas de quoi manger*.

R

ROFFE

Rough, tough. As in: *un ch'min roffe*, a rough road; *c'est roffe*, that's tough.

RULE 19. It Takes Two To Tangle.

The chief characteristic of Standard French is its ceremonial quality. As any former language student will recall from his schooldays, French is what is in the book. Conversely, if it's not in the book, it isn't French. On this cardinal point the whole elaborate structure of the noble French language has been built.

This principle is sustained by the weight of the French Academy whose *Dictionnaire* lets in only so many words every year, and also by generations of French teachers who fail anyone who doesn't do as he's told. Finally the whole thing is tied together by a decree of the French Minister of Public Instruction dated February 26, 1901, which makes it illegal to speak anything but what the Government says you can.

By contrast to all this formality and rigidity, joual is free form. There are rules, as we have seen, but there is no penalty for breaking them; no one ever flunked joual. This may, of course, change if the people's language ever falls into the hands of schoolteachers.

An important rule has been enunciated above. It requires the use of metathesis, that is, the tangling or mangling of successive sounds in a word wherever possible. And lest anyone thinks that joual speakers are being criticized for following this rule, he should remember that the same thing often happens in English: *hasp* is merely a tangled form of the earlier *haepse*, just as clasp used to be *clapse*, *thrill* was once *thirl*, and so on.

Thus the strict application of Rule 19 obliges a joual speaker to say *escousse* rather than the French form **secousse*, and *ermise* for French **remise*. Rule 19 even applies to monosyllables, where it has the effect of reversing them. Thus joual watchers may encounter *ej'* for French **je*, as in: *ej' vais aller*; or *el'* instead of French **le*, as in: *el' fils à Jean*, 'John's boy.'

One could multiply these examples but for our purpose they suffice to illustrate the corollary of Rule 19: joual is what is *not* in the book.

S

STE. KATRINNE

Main thoroughfare in downtown Mont Ray-all. It is divided transversely into *Ste. Katrinne esse*, the joual half, and *Ste. Katrinne ouesse*, the Anglo half. The twain touch in the middle but never meet.

ST. TSITTE

Town in Champlain County, NE of *Trois Riviéres*, *q.v.* Pronounce to rhyme with 'flit.' Cf. **St. Tite*.

SAVOUÉRE

See *s'ché*. Cf. French **savoir*.

S'CHÉ

First person singular of *savouére*, 'to know.' Pronounce rather like 'sshay.' As in: *S'ché pâ* (in Canajan: 'I dough no'). Cf. French **je sais*.

SCHKOOT ME

City in Schkoot Me District, lying almost due north of Kay Beck City.

S'LICHER

An invitation to visit His Satanic Majesty. As in: *Liche-toé!* (in Canajan: 'Goat tha devil!').

SLOCHE

Slush. Pronounce to rhyme with 'boche.' As in: *C'est pâ marchab' à cause d'la sloche* (in Canajan: 'Sarda walk fur the slush'). Cf. French *neige à demi fondue*.

S'PÂ

Adverbial phrase inviting assent. As in: *'Vous v'nez, s'pâ?'* (in Canajan: 'Yer cummin, arn'cha?'). Cf. French **n'est-ce pas*.

S'QUI

The interrogative pronoun 'what?' Pronounce like 'ski.' As in: *s'qui est arrivé?* (in Canajan: 'Wha hopp'n?'). Cf. French **qu'est-ce qui*.

STIMPE

Postage stamp. Pronounce to rhyme with *grimpe*. As in: *A-tsu des stimpes de witt cennes?* (in Canajan: 'Yagoddiny aid cent stamps?') Cf. French **timbre-poste*.

SWIRE

Evening, night. As in: *j't'v'rai à swire* (in Canajan: 'seeya tnite'). Cf. French **soir*.

T

TALON, JEAN

The first and greatest Intendant of Nooph Rance, Talon in a few short years helped put the colony back on its feet after the ruinous Irk Wah wars, conducted the first Canajan census (2034 men, 1181 women), granted seigniories to all his French friends, and invented the zipper.

To his lasting credit Talon also broke the Briddish monopoly of the infamous liquor trade among the Indians. This came about because in the Briddish colonies to the south, many furt raiders used to get the Indians drunk and then take their pelts away from them, a practice known as scalping (see *Furt Raid*).

In Nooph Rance the selling or giving of liquor to Indians had always been punishable by a heavy fine and, for the second offence, whipping or banishment. While this did not entirely prevent scalping it helped discourage it, thus putting the French Canajans at a considerable commercial disadvantage. The Irk Wah were deemed sufficiently punished by hangovers and the loss of their pelts. As a result much conflict arose between the civil and religious authorities, between making money and saving souls.

Talon saw a way to solve the moral issue by shifting the

penalty from the wrongdoer to the victim, thus showing himself to be well ahead of his time in penal reform. By an Ordinance of 1668 Talon permitted all Canajans to sell or give liquor to the Indians, thus making the Canajans competitive with the unscrupulous Briddish furt raiders. At the same time, to protect Indians from the curse of drunkenness, Talon added a rider sternly forbidding them from getting drunk under penalty of a fine of two beavers and public exposure in the pillory.

Almost overnight the flagging economy of the little colony revived. New liquor outlets opened everywhere, the number of beaver pelts in circulation doubled, while the constant need for new pillories kept the colony's 36 carpenters working overtime.

At first the Indians were much puzzled about how they had suddenly become the guilty parties, but in time they came to have a better appreciation of the Canajan legal system.

TANNANT(E)

Unlike *tanné*, *q.v.*, which connotes exhaustion or boredom, *tannant* is uphill all the way. As in: *un tannant de beau châr*: a terrific car; *une tannante de robe*: a swell dress.

TANNÉ

Tired out, exhausted. As in: *Chus tanné* (in Canajan: 'I'm beat').

'Chus tanné.'

TCHOMME

Boyfriend, buddy. Cf. French *camarade*.

TÉVÉ

Television. As in: *'Hé, Man! 'coute la tévé!'* (in Canajan: 'Hey, Mom! lookit the teevee!'). Cf. French *télé*.

TOO-SWITT

Immediately. As in: *Faites-lé too-switt* (in Canajan: 'Doot ride away'). Cf. French *tout de suite*.

TOUJOUS

Always. Pronounce to rhyme with 'yoohoo.' Cf. French *toujours*.

TROIS RIVIÉRES

The second-oldest city in Canada. Jock Car Chay visited the site of Trois Riviéres in 1535, but the city itself was founded in 1634 by Sham Plane. Later investigators have been able to locate only one river, however (the St. Mauriss), the other two rivers having apparently disappeared in the meantime. Either that or somebody wasn't very good at arithmetic (See *Counting*).

Riviéres is pronounced to rhyme more or less with 'chivy ire.'

TSU

The second person singular pronoun, i.e., 'you,' occurs in two forms in joual just as it does in Standard French, so the joual speaker need not feel short-changed. The nominative form is *tsu*, as in: *tsu la vois?* (in Canajan: 'dja sear?'). Cf. French **tu*. The objective form is *toé* (pronounce something like 'tway') as in: *couche-toé!* (in Canajan: 'lay down!'). Cf. French **toi*. For a discussion of joual personal pronouns, see *Moé*.

T'TALEUR

After a short time. As in: *J'irai t'taleur* (in Canajan: 'Allgo soon'). Cf. French **tout à l'heure.*

U

UNILINGUISME

Besides being hard to pronounce, this term is difficult for most Anglos to understand. For generations their Kay Beck *has* been unilingual, i.e., English, and they are appalled at the thought that any democratically elected government would want to make it *unilingue* in French. Such a policy flies in the face of more than 200 years of Canajan history and has to be unsound.

As we have already noted (see *Introduction*), both sides are so embedded in history that they have lost touch with current reality. If, as independent tests prove conclusively, a majority of Kay Beckers speak joual, just as a majority of Anglos speak Canajan, then the ancient battle in the province between French and English has not merely been lost: it has become irrelevant. It matters naught whether the government decrees that French shall be the *langue de travail*, or the *langue d'instruction*, or even, Wessmount, *q.v.*, notwithstanding, the *langue officielle*. Increasingly French and English Kay Beckers will go right on speaking joual or Canajan (as the case may be) whatever the law says.

One point should not escape notice: anyone who is not able to acquit himself in either of these two languages will just have to

take his lumps. This conclusion follows inevitably from the fact
that the population of Kay Beck is made up of Anglos, jouals and
ethnics — the last-named coming from Ethnicstan, the ancestral
homeland of all Canajans who speak with a foreign accent.
Formerly ethnics were obliged to speak broken English. With the
trend towards unilingualism in Kay Beck, they will soon be
required to speak broken French instead.

UNIVARSTÉ

Educational institution. As in: *A suit les cours à l'univarsté* (in
Canajan: 'Sheeze taken a corset th' yune versty'). Cf. French
université.

V

VIVE LA DIFFÉRENCE

The *raison* of Kay Beck's *être*, or possibly the *sine qua* of her *non*, is said to be that she is not a province like the others. If she were, what would there be left to talk about?

This concept is by no means as revolutionary as Kay Beckers would have us believe. It is, in fact, part of the Canadian quiddity that *no* province is like the others, for while some provinces are more like the others and other provinces are less like the others, other provinces are not at all like the others. It really boils down to this, that if no province is like the others (and how could it be?), then all are in some sense the same, or at any rate in the same boat. Being in the same boat is, in fact, the essence of Federalism.

But the leaders of Kay Beck were not to be put off by such constitutional sophistries. They argued quite convincingly that while some provinces might be islands and other provinces peninsulas, only Kay Beck was P.Q. No other province could make that claim.

Besides (they argued at the last Federal-Provincial conference), wasn't it true that joual, the national language of Kay Beck, was not a language like the others? And if Kay Beck did not have a language like the others, it could not be a province like the others. *Quod erat demonstrandum*.

Here it must be admitted that they were on shaky ground. For secret studies by the National Research Council, some of which form the basis of the present work, confirm the close similarity between joual and Canajan, the two national languages of Canada (see *Introduction*). Indeed, it is a demonstrable fact that just as Canajan is Anglo joual, so joual is French Canajan. They are, in a very real sense, mirror images of each other.

At this point, of necessity, matters rest until the next Federal-Provincial conference when, it may be predicted, they will not advance appreciably.

VOCRI

To hunt for and bring back (something). Pronounce 'voe cree.' As in: *Vocri son coat* (in Canajan: 'Glook friz jackit'). Cf. French *Va quérir son veston*.

VOT'

Second person plural form of the possessive pronoun (in Canajan: 'yer'). See *Not'*. Cf. French *votre*.

VOYAGE, AVOUÉRE SON

To be fed up, to have had the course. As in: *J'ai mon voyage*: I've had it.

W

WATCHER

To watch, look out for. Pronounce 'wah chay.' As in: *watch-toé!*
(in Canajan: 'watchit!'). Cf. French *attention!*

WESSMOUNT

Non-joual part of the City of Mont Ray-all. Ancestral preserve of
the Anglos, *q.v.*

X

XAMINER

To examine, look into something. Pronounce 'gzaminay.' As in: *J'l'ai pâ xaminé* (in Canajan: 'I dint zamine it'). Cf. French *examiner*.

XEMPE

Example, instance. Pronounce 'gzempe.' As in: *par xempe* (in Canajan: 'frintstants'). Cf. French *exemple*.

Y

Y

He, they. Pronounce to rhyme with 'wee.' See *A*. Cf. French *il*.

YI

Him, to him. Pronounce 'yee.' As in: *A yi dzit* (in Canajan: 'She sedtim'). Cf. French *lui*.

YOÙ

Where, in what direction. Pronounce 'you.' As in: *Yoù vâs-tsu?* (in Canajan: 'Wear'ya goyne?'). Cf. French *où*.

Bickerstaff